Chapters of Your Life

**Wise Words for Women
On A
Life-Changing Journey**

M. AUDREY STEWART-HINCHCLIFFE

RESOURCE *Publications* · Eugene, Oregon

Chapters of Your Life
Wise Words for Women On A Life-Changing Journey

Published in 2021 by Arawak Publications and Resource Publications

© M. Audrey Stewart-Hinchcliffe 2021. All rights reserved.

COVID-19 derived character and place names:

Comorbidia: a sleepy little town on the outskirts of the parish of Pandemia in Virusha (Comorbidities)
Controla: the pastor of the village church (Control)
Covidence: a village in Pandemia (COVID-19)
Infecta: the village bar (Infection)
Isolatine: the market on outskirts of Covidence (Isolation)
Maas Que: Protie Peckham's paramour (Quarantine)
North Vaccinia: a mountainous area of Virusha known for its picturesque hills and valleys / ideal for pilgrimages (Vaccine)
Pandemia: a parish in the country of Virusha (Pandemic)
Protie Peckham: the protagonist (Protocol)
Virusha: the country in which the story is set (Virus)

© M. Audrey Stewart-Hinchcliffe 2021.

> This edition licensed by special permission of Arawak publications, Kingston, Jamaica

ISBN 978-1-6667-3410-2 (paperback)
ISBN 978-1-6667-2961-0 (eBook)

25 24 23 22 21
 e   d   c   b   a

Credits
- Original blooms from the garden of M. Audrey Stewart-Hinchcliffe
- Design and arrangement by Ayo Ledgerwood

CONTENTS

Dedication	iv
Foreword *by* Mariame McIntosh Robinson	v
Acknowledgments	vii
CUTTING TIES	1
LETTING GO	5
TRANSITIONING	10
THE JOURNEY	13
WELCOME TO YOUR NEW LIFE	18
THE NEW BEGINNING	21
COURAGE AND CONTROL	23
THE POWER TO TAKE CHARGE	25
FEELING OF FREEDOM	27
THE MIDDLE GROUND	30
THE NEW LIFE – HERE AND NOW	33
ENDURANCE	36
SELF-ACCEPTANCE	38
GRATITUDE AND APPRECIATION	40
THE REALITIES OF A NEW LIFE	43
FULFILLMENT AND BALANCE	46
THE END OF OUR USEFUL UTILITY	49
SHADOWS AND SILHOUETTES ACROSS OUR NEW LIFE	53

DEDICATION

What a privilege to dedicate this book to the memory of my trusted co-worker, colleague and friend, Kareen Foster-Jones,
who was snatched away by COVID-19.

To the members of M'Power Women's Group of which she was a founding member,
thank you for being a blessing to me.

God's hand is at work in our lives.

FOREWORD

As COVID-19 continues to wreak havoc on the world in various obvious and subtle ways, Chapters of Your Life is a well-timed inspirational read for people of all backgrounds. It provides a practical outlook on how to successfully cope with the momentous changes happening around us. The author has delivered a relatable page-turner that will leave you pondering life after completing the book.

While the plot at face value is packed with intrigue in a succinct narrative, embedded are deeper meanings that may cause you to pause and reflect as you savour the storyline as it unfolds. It is hard to not be jolted to action to live your best life after reading this book.

The story is about a middle-aged woman who has been living a comfortable life, of good standing in her community, with some power and influence, a level of independence that may make some envious, and an unshakeable relationship with the Lord. She has a spiritual awakening, which some may informally regard as a symptom of midlife crisis, as she goes on a journey in pursuit of her best, authentic life. It is interesting to note how much easier it is for persons without the many perceived worldly possessions or obligations (e.g. a mortgage, children, etc.) to make changes in their lives to truly pursue their passions.

Protie, the main character, was able to make this spiritual journey and transformation more easily than

Foreword

her peers who were stuck in unhappy marriages, looking after children, and tending to work demands.

The author challenges us to ask ourselves how "stuck" are we and what work do we need to do in order to release ourselves to live our most authentic lives. The book also forces us to come to terms with questions such as: "What role does religion or having a strong spiritual foundation play in giving us the clarity and courage to recognize the changes we need to make in our lives?" Protie did not miss the advertisement on TV, while most did as they went about their busy, routine oriented lives. In addition, the reader is challenged to answer: "What role, if any, does middle-age have in our receptiveness and openness to change? Does it help or hinder?"

Chapters of Your Life is a "self-help" guide that provides specific suggestions on how to both cope with the immediate crisis of positively navigating this pandemic and its effects, while at the same time creating a life that is purposeful and continuously evolving.

One of the treasures of reading books by this author is the memorable quotes she includes in her writings. This book is no different.

The author presents these nuggets to women in particular as a special keepsake as we navigate life's expected challenges.

Mariame McIntosh Robinson
PRESIDENT AND CEO
FIRST GLOBAL BANK, JAMAICA

ACKNOWLEDGMENTS

Behind every book are persons who participate in or situations which contribute to bringing it to life.

Strange as it may sound, the situation which inspired the writing of this book was the coronavirus pandemic during which the author was consigned to home due to age and comorbidities. In this regard, it allowed time for reflection on life as a woman who has trod the path of the main character.

As usual, my trusted assistant, Yolande Sealy, rose to the occasion at short notice to type and organize the book sections. It is remarkable that she did so while in isolation at home suffering from COVID-19. Hence, acknowledging her is special.

What would I have done without my sounding board Dr Canute Thompson whose comments and suggestions led to the addition of book sections to provide a more complete journey in the life of the main character Protie Peckham.

I pay tribute to Mariame Robinson for her Foreword. Mariame offers us her uniquely penetrating perspective, highlighting the importance of the lessons and issues that present "life's expected challenges".

My Publisher Pansy Benn offered her shoulder on which to lean as without her advice I would have gone off on a tangent and the book would never have been completed.

To all the women, and men too, who will read what I am calling my "Little Inspirational Book" — I hope you will be as inspired as I was writing it.

Cutting TIES

Journeys have a beginning and an end. Some journeys are planned and some are thrust upon us. Some are physical, some are emotional, and in some cases we don't even realize a journey has begun, hence we have no idea when or how it will end. Such is the case of Protie Peckham, a middle-aged woman from the village of Covidence, in the parish of Pandemia, in the country of Virusha. The country is mountainous – particularly in the area of North Vaccinia, which is known for its picturesque views of hills and valleys and as an ideal place for a pilgrimage.

The idea of leaving Covidence occurred to Protie one night when she saw an advertisement on her black and white television encouraging middle-aged women to join a group of Christian middle-aged women on a pilgrimage to a resort in the mountains of North Vaccinia. The women would have various means of transportation at their disposal, and the journey would include long walks and overnight stays in several villages. At each stop, they would eat, meditate and pray and, of course, there would be lamentations of love lost and found. Protie was instantly inspired to heed the call, and it was at one of these stops on the seventh night that Protie had a dream which would change the course of her life forever.

Protie was leaving home for the first time to go far afield at the ripe middle age of forty-seven. Before then she had only left the village to go shopping at nearby Isolatine, where she also went to school up to the seventh grade. So, to go on a pilgrimage must be an unimaginable feat!

Protie never got married and never had children but was suspected of having secret dalliances particularly with one Maas Que, also unmarried, but the father of seven children with three different women. This situation was always of concern to her as Maas Que always told her she was the special one as she cost him nothing by way of support. Her support came from the legacy left to her by her grandparents, and a meagre wage from the Post Office, her first and only place of employment.

She was always independent, hence she did not feel obligated to report to anyone that she was going on a pilgrimage.

So off she went while the village was still asleep.

Chapters of Your Life

Letting GO

Back home in Covidence, Maas Que was having thoughts about the times spent with Protie. He came to the realization that what he was feeling was a profound longing for their infrequent trysts. Thoughts of her brought flutters in his chest and heat in his loins. What was worse, she never told him goodbye, and he had no idea where she was gone, or whether she was ever coming back. This troubled him greatly, as already there was the whisper in the village that maybe she was gone to become a nun. This was puzzling to him as his little exposure to religion taught him that it took a special kind of woman to become a nun, and he did not see Protie fitting into this mould.

Maas Que was overcome with grief as he felt he was being punished for having dalliances with a virtuous woman and never "made a woman of her". He reasoned that marriage was part of a woman's journey, and the mothers of his children had raised the question a number of times. Despite this, however, Protie never did – not even once. So he thought that her leaving was a sign that he had misread cues that he should have been married, and to no other woman but Protie. But now she was gone.

The place for solace at Covidence was either. the church or "The Infecta", as the village bar was fondly dubbed. This was on Friday, one whole week since Protie disappeared. In the evening after a full day at work at the stone quarry and after collecting his week's pay, Maas Que headed to "The Infecta" along with Quinn, Boo and Seltzer, his boyhood friends – and together they talked about their escapades. The three always marvelled at how the best looking one among them managed to stay single. The other two were miserable in marriages in which they felt trapped with aging wives and wayward children. Que's children were no better, but he was not saddled with them as he kept them and their mothers at bay with what little financial support he could afford to give them. His friends knew about his seeming affair with Protie, but never knew she had left the district unknown to everyone.

As they sat on the stone bench outside the bar with cold beers in hand, Que began to unburden himself of the torment he was experiencing caused by Protie's disappearance. His ego was more hurt than any feeling for her from his heart. He lamented to his buddies that Protie's disappearance had left him sad and weary, and that was the reason he was drinking – more like gulping – and drowning himself in beer. For every one they drank, he gulped down three. This made him tipsy and talkative. Protie had really messed with his headspace, and he was only now feeling the pains of separation from a woman. He never had this feeling of emptiness before.

Maas Que started to cry.

Quinn, Boo and Seltzer were extremely surprised at the way he openly lamented how he felt about Protie but never told her, choosing rather to suppress his feelings as he felt he was incapable of making a commitment to anyone. He was now soliciting their help in tracking her down. They pledged to help their friend embark on this mission – although they had no idea where to begin. They just wanted to stop him from crying as this was the first time they were witnessing a big man cry. The trio promised him they would come up with a plan although they had a strong sense one would never materialize.

> *"May the petals teach me the*
> *art of letting go"*
> – Xan Oku
> (https://ifunny.co...may-the-petals-teach-me)

TRANSITIONING

Saturday dawned in Covidence and the usual group of women, with their miserable children, assembled to board the rickety country bus to go to market at Isolatine. But someone was missing. It was Protie Peckham, secretly referred to as the "barren one" – as she was the only woman among them who had no offspring. While some envied her, others loathed her . . . for, how could she be with Maas Que who left everyone who slept with him with a pickney?! They felt she "chruo-we" hers. The fact is they would really never know what she did when she was with Que – and now she is missing. What will happen at church tomorrow if she does not show up? She was the pillar of the "Wash Foot Church", which held Sunday morning service in the old school house. Pastor

Controla had his eyes on Protie, but knew better than to even try his luck as he feared Maas Que's wrath. Little did he know that she had feelings for him too. His weekly fiery sermons sent the congregation into a frenzy and it was not unusual for female members to have multiple self-induced orgasms – Protie among them.

So, what would make her disappear, leaving no message behind or not saying goodbye? Sunday came ... All day, speculation was rife that Maas Que had a hand in her disappearance, but his buddies defended him stoutly, citing his lamenting and crying at the bar during their drinking spree Friday after work. The thought of Maas Que crying – the tough guy he was known to be – made the speculators beat a hasty retreat.

But Monday morning came ... Unruly children hopping, skipping and jumping on their way to school gave no thought to the missing person they all called Auntie. But the parents kept up their tongue-wagging, with all sorts of tales about the missing one. One thing was certain. Protie had to be found.

A village is a hive of glass,
where nothing unobserved can pass.
– Charles Spurgeon
(Quotefancy.com)

The JOURNEY

Covidence and North Vaccinia were never mentioned in the same sentence until the advertisement about the pilgrimage appeared. Since television was not very common in the village, it is not known how many of the inhabitants would have seen the advertisement which may have been shown perhaps just once that week on a Tuesday night when even those with television sets were too busy cooking dinner on their coal stove, or on an open fire in the backyard. This was normal life in deep rural Covidence. Covidians' life was one of farming, market vending, school and church. The men were wild, the women had babies and a few of the children worked hard in school to escape the routine and avoid becoming like their parents. The upstanding people were the teachers, the postmaster, the sanitary inspector, the district constable, the pastor and usually a successful farmer dubbed "the village governor". Protie was the postal clerk; religious to the core of her being – which explains why she was led to watch the weekly short programme from a foreign church beckoning her to the pilgrimage.

Protie made the journey to meet up with other Christian middle-aged women. A bus picked her up on the outskirts of Pandemia in the sleepy little town of Comorbidia. Here sits the bus station from which anything on wheels takes travellers to the end of the dirt road when travelling to villages in the hills of North Vaccinia. Having met up with her companions, Protie was now at the beginning of her pilgrimage. After the meet and greet, the prayers and a hearty meal, the journey began.

She wondered if she had done the right thing to leave her beloved district of Covidence without saying goodbye even to Maas Que and Pastor Controla. A feeling of fear washed over her as she looked around to see that she was surrounded by a bunch of loud singing, hand-clapping, sweating, overweight women who could just as well have been on their way to a fat farm rather than a religious pilgrimage. She broke into a sweat, which was more than she was used to as a result of early menopause. She took a deep breath and composed herself; after all, she needed the experience of the pilgrimage to test her faith in her religion which kept her a virtuous woman. No one would ever know that for all the time she spent with Maas Que, she remained a virgin – although, at times of intense arousal, her screams of "Lord God! Jesus Christ!" led him to think she might have been reliving her experiences with other men she had been with, as "God" and "Christ" meant nothing to him by way of religion considering that he was illiterate and never went to church. Most of the time they spent together, she taught him the alphabet.

Protie settled in her seat and, despite the voices of her newly found sisters and noise from the rickety old bus, she fell asleep.

Sweet dream or revelation, the journey began not only on the road but even more so through her life. In her dream she saw a road sign, "Welcome to Your Life". A new journey, nowhere near the one she signed up for, had begun.

*Protie's journey
is now our journey too.*

Welcome to Your NEW LIFE

Protie's life is your life. It's my life. It's the life from which we escaped through the years by putting in its place things, stuff, fillers and constant movement from one stage of our existence to another. At some time, some of us wake up to wonder: Where have the years gone? They didn't go. We were the ones who drowned ourselves out and took the years with us. At some point, like Protie Peckham, we will have to face a similar unusual occurrence while on a pilgrimage for a certain experience which we thought would be good for a middle-aged, religious woman. Religion aside, at some time or other, as women we all need to take ourselves on that pilgrimage and in a dream see the road sign "Welcome to Your Life".

The journey has just begun to find our true self – our new life.

The starting point is the realization of the three phases of life that we have to come to terms with – we are born, we live, and we die. The beginning and the end we have little or no control over; it is in the middle – how we live – that we will be judged by. Our words, our deeds, and our emotions have driven us to the present moment when we have to pause and confront ourselves. This was the realization that sent Protie Peckham on the pilgrimage to the mountains of North Vaccinia. We all have dreams to be fulfilled; we have to expand our mind – and the achievement and success we so earnestly pursued may turn out to be the cause of our unfulfillment, as we never confronted ourselves until that point in our middle age when, like Protie, an emptiness flows over our being. We realize we are lonely and unhappy.

A pilgrimage through self beckons.

The new BEGINNING

"When we admit our mistakes and make amends for them, we reclaim our power and actually like ourselves better."
–Steve Gilliland
(https://quotefancy.com/)

One of the ways of finding oneself is to admit that we have been doing too many of the wrong things. In this regard, we need to call a halt, sit down, take a deep breath and make a list of the unnecessary things we have done and got so immersed in that we forgot who we really are. This is akin to Protie's pilgrimage.

Next, make another list of what our new life will be like – the new life we will welcome ourselves to. Don't beat ourselves up about the past life; rather, forgive ourselves for the mistakes we made, ask forgiveness of those we hurt or neglected, and learn from the past as we embark on the new life.

*Be true to yourself.
Step back from all the noise and
make a roadmap for your life.*

Courage And CONTROL

Protie Peckham had the courage to depart Covidence on a pilgrimage that would take her to find her new life. Her courage to do so is found in all women who believe we have done too much to create a life which we no longer enjoy, such as the life of a middle-aged woman of forty-seven years. The thought of half a century of a life looming – turning 50 in just a few years – drove a level of fear into Protie that propelled her decision to set off on the pilgrimage. The sweat of menopause is cleansing to the soul, and the anxiety is that of a woman who viewed her new life – the approach of the next half century. Will we like our new life? Will our colleagues like us in our new life? What if we're not good enough for the world?

These questions will be resolved as we take control of the belief in our new self.

The power to Take CHARGE

The new life gave you power over you. To be in charge of you, means owning you and you don't have to let go to no one else. Covidence thought it owned Protie Peckham but she took off without leaving a trace. Covidians now do not have her to badmouth and link her with Maas Que. Will she return as the Postal Clerk they knew, or will she ever return, if at all, a transformed woman. Whatever happens, she has taken charge of herself and took off to the mountains of North Vaccinia, feeling no obligation to have informed not even her best friend Maas Que. This power to take charge can be triggered by a simple advertisement on an old black and white television. Who would have thought this was possible? Nonetheless, it appealed to Protie and she answered the call.

The difference between taking control and taking charge of our lives is having the ability not to give in to what others think of us or want us to be. What they think of us does not really matter anymore.

The power to take charge of ourselves is liberating.

Feeling of FREEDOM

Feeling makes us human. Yet we do not express our feeling that we have lost ourself by middle age. Instead we bottle it up behind an impenetrable façade. Hiding our feelings make us seem always so cool, the one everyone wants to be with. So it was with Protie Peckham. She was the go-to person at the Post Office, she was the backbone of the church, the one Controla depended on and had dreams of humping one day. But freedom beckoned on the television screen, and it sensitized Protie to the possibilities outside of Covidence and into the mountains of North Vaccinia.

Freedom to travel to the outskirts of the sleepy town of Comorbidia and freedom to board that rickety bus . . . It took her all those years, through to the ripe old age of forty-seven, to spread her wings. She now saw it as being free from her parish of Pandemia, in the country of Virusha.

How free do we feel among our peers, soaring in our career, owning money, power, influence, things, stuff of all kinds, and absorbed in our popularity? We live on a high till one day we realize we are trapped in middle age with the next half-century in the offing. Our lifespan is the marker, perhaps with a touch of comorbidities (the presence of multiple diseases in the same person); we realize the time for freedom is now. We must seize the right to act, think and choose. We are no longer imprisoned or enslaved in our importance.

Like Protie, we eventually choose to be free and to no more answer to anyone but ourselves.

The middle GROUND

Let's raise a toast to the new-found life over which we now have control, and to the freedom to be who we want to be! But it is how we live this phase of life that will determine if we are rewarded and remembered, and if someone will eulogize us with the words: "Well done, good and faithful servant" (Matthew 23:25) – and it will be sincere.

The new life will drive our sense of purpose for service and success. With the half-century approaching, we will be tempted to hurry through this period, but instead we need to find a middle ground with a roadmap setting out our approach to the last stages of life. Death is certain but we don't have to hurry to give it effect.

This is perhaps what Protie Peckham was doing on the pilgrimage to the mountains of North Vaccinia – mapping out the new life that she will have control over. She can go home again if she chooses – to the post office and the church; she may choose as well to remain in a vacuum-like state of mind; or follow one of her new-found middle-aged friends back to her hometown. She will have to challenge herself with a new level of thinking, thereby motivating herself, and perhaps after deep contemplation, map a whole new future.

The best approach will be to find a middle ground. Back to the old way of life is not an option. The new-found freedom will not be relinquished, so a middle ground between the former life and freedom to craft a new life places us in a comfort zone where power, courage and control will co-exist.

What is certain is that from now on always be in charge of our new life with gratitude for and joyfulness in our success and happiness. Our self-worth will be priceless and it will be time for self-affirmation and celebration. As Protie discovers, the middle ground is solid ground and, together with her new-found middle-aged friends, she can sing and shout: "On Christ the solid rock I stand. All other ground is sinking sand" (Robert Critchley, *A Harvest of Songs*, 2007).

The middle ground is stabilizing and serves as the jumping-off point for acceptance of the new life.

The NEW LIFE – Here and Now

The feeling of having our feet on solid ground is truly liberating. We are in a new place, encumbered only by getting in our own way. Being independent and self-sufficient allows us to move at our own pace in this new life. We are free to make choices and when we make mistakes, to learn from them so long as those mistakes are not damaging and irreparable.

There will be circumstances which open the door to opportunities, but there will also be challenges. Our sense of determination will propel us to heights previously unthinkable. New experiences will test the new life, the new self. We can decide which direction to take our new self. The best way is to gather information on those who have taken a similar path and have left a legacy of power and influence that impact society positively. The new life is not worth living if influence and power are misused and wasted.

From time to time it is worth reflecting on the former life and determining what you would have liked from someone as a role model then. Perhaps such a situation did exist but you were unaware of it at the time. Whatever qualities you would have liked modelled then, be prepared to impart those now to someone along the path of your new life's journey.

Building your legacy has begun.

Self-discipline and humility go a long way in achieving success. The companion to success is failure; so is risk and so is

The NEW LIFE – Here and Now

reward. What we practise, how we are seen, will inform the content of our eulogy. Therefore, doing the right things in this new life should be the aim of a life well lived.

> *"Well done, thou good and
> faithful servant…"*

ENDURANCE

The new life must be sustained; it must be nourished to withstand the rigours of power and influence. The world will be looking at you as you execute the new life. It means that endurance must underpin moves into the future with its uncharted goals and objectives. At the heart of endurance is age. For example, at the age of 50 years onward, our attitude to life will be key. We will have to draw on past experience, choosing to build on what worked, and to embrace change – simply put, the goals that propelled Protie to depart the former life, the courage and faith to take the journey and never look back. This strength of character allowed her to endure the journey to North Vaccinia, to endure the experience of steady soul-searching, and to arrive at the

ENDURANCE

decision on her new life.

This is the same strength of character, courage and faith which will be needed as we journey through the new life. You can bet there will be questions, temptations, trials and challenges. Endurance will be the bedrock of the new life.

Be inspirational. Share your story.

Self- ACCEPTANCE

We begin by knowing ourselves. Our self-confidence comes from the road map we put in place for living our new life. As time goes by, we will have flashbacks to the life back in Covidence. As boring as it may appear now, it gave Protie Peckham a platform from which to depart on the pilgrimage induced by that television advertisement.

Fast forward from the journey, the dream on that rickety old bus, the soul-searching, and now acceptance of the self and the new life. We feel secure knowing we are at peace with the plan for the new life; hence nothing can shake our confidence. There's no room for external influence. We know who we are so we are not defined by anyone or seduced by

Self-ACCEPTANCE

temptations coming our way. Our life's plan, with the right actions which we will live by, signals that we are who we are, and in good time our acquaintances will accept the new you because you have demonstrated that you have accepted yourself. This will keep you grounded wherever you choose to reside, while the old life back in the district of Covidence fades from our consciousness.

Raise a toast to self-acceptance!

Gratitude And APPRECIATION

Gratitude for the new life is a component of a larger whole, other elements of which include knowledge and skills, attitudes and habits. Choose the one that will most likely make the new life sustainable and from experience this will become habit – and this is how you will live your best life spontaneously as a daily experience.

In order to get through the day from your waking moment to the last thing you do at night, a habit must be effortless and fun-filled. It is what works for you and does not mimic what someone else does, nor does it presume that it is a one-size-fits-all programme or activity. It is what you do almost as a rite of passage. It is who you are in this new life.

Establish your own guiding principles –

for gratitude for being a child of God. You are you. You are unique in this new life. What you have become must be the basis for gratitude and appreciation to those around you who have added value to your life.

Make a daily list of what you are grateful for – as this will be the marker for the success of your new life.

Develop a daily habit list – Each day be pre-pared to take advantage of opportunities to cultivate a lasting habit.

You must develop the capacity to withstand difficulties and to recover quickly. Make resilience a habit, for one never knows what lies around the corner and, like anyone else, you too will be faced with problems or adversities of one sort or another. Such problems may be related to work, health, family and other relationships, finances or other stressors; and adversities may take the form of trauma, tragedy, threats and suchlike.

It is useful to look in the rear-view mirror

from time to time – from Covidence, to the pilgrimage to the mountains of North Vaccinia, to the new "anywhere-in-the-world" address you've chosen. You are now blooming where you plant yourself. The stronger the root stock, the more beautiful the bloom. The choice will be whether you are for cutting to be inserted in a bouquet or a potted plant – in which case you will wither and die; or whether you grow with deep roots into the ground – in which case you will survive changes in the weather and quickly spring back to grow and bloom.

... a habit must be effortless and fun-filled. It is what you do almost as a rite of passage.

The realities Of A NEW LIFE

The meaning of a new life for Protie Peckham – whose life is my life, and is also your life – brings reality into sharp focus. A new life means you move from one place to another, or to another country. It also means a change of career, or recovery from an unpleasant experience.

Dan Matthews, Certified Psychosocial Rehabilitation Practitioner (CPRP), offers his advice about how to start a new life without sacrificing everything you have (see https://www.lifehack. org/. . . start-new-life.html. Updated May 2021). Protie may have been ahead of her time as her story, my story, our story about finding a new life is patterned along the lines of the twelve changes Matthews outlines.

The realities of a new life force us to look in the rear-view mirror while forging ahead with living our best lives. We must never forget where we are coming from, where we are now and where we are heading. As previously mentioned, life has three phases – we are born, we live, and then we die. The only phase we have control over is how we live. How, when and where we are born contributes to how we live, but we are solely responsible for our waning days culminating in disability and death. We cannot now go back. The easy part is retirement – but it is nonetheless important to decide from what and when.

A stark reminder of life's phases is set out in Chinese novelist Zhou Daxin's latest novel, *The Sky Gets Dark, Slowly* (2020): Aging creeps up slowly, and we must face the realities that come with it sooner rather than later – "because in always waiting for later, we can lose the best moments . . ."

The realities Of A NEW LIFE

What is your reality?

So, here's to all the Protie Peckhams! Now all that is left for you to do is to live the best life you can. "Problems and pain are inevitable, but prayers and faith in God are always the best solution" (www.facebook/page/Dewdrops).

*A new life for Protie –
whose life is also your life – brings reality
into sharp focus.*

Fulfillment And BALANCE

We make choices in our lives and sometimes regret those choices. But what we have to strive for in this new life is balance. As you do this, it is useful to be guided by the following:

• Get out of your own way. Have faith in what you can do and do it. That will help to overcome the fear of failure.

• You must believe in your God-given abilities and in yourself. And even if you fail, remember that failure, too, can become a stepping stone to phenomenal growth and even greater success.

• Get out of your comfort zone – take calculated risks and celebrate the outcome.

Fulfillment And BALANCE

- Decide what you want to do and whether you can do it alone, and if you can't, decide what kind of support you need – e.g., a counsellor, a mentor, or just to hear from others who have already trod the path you are now on.

- Develop a hunger for knowledge: Read and research in order to develop fresh ideas and shape relevant solutions to issues and incidents in your life.

- Take on tasks that no one else wants and assert your superior self.

- Display a solid life's philosophy.

- Make yourself visible and relevant but not officiously so.

And finally, I commend these words from the English writer Samuel Johnson (1709-1784) as you live the new life:

Chapters of Your Life

> *"Exert you talents and distinguish yourself, and don't think of retiring from the world until the world will be sorry that you retire."*
> (https://quotefancy.com/)

The end of our USEFUL UTILITY

Protie Peckham was staring down the ripe middle age of half a century – perhaps with some fear and trepidation. But she took comfort in the fact that at nearly 50 she was secure in her inherited resources, in reasonable health and in her strong faith in God.

However, life throws Protie a curve ball that she could not have anticipated would be just around the corner waiting to knock her block off. Enter the coronavirus pandemic. In the past she may have endured a little chest cold which was quickly cleared up by a cup of ginger, sinkle bible or turmeric tea. A few times this chest cold would develop into the flu with the full body blow, but nothing that home remedies and a few Panadols could not take care of. However, as she approached the age of fifty years, Protie found the affliction took longer each time to get rid of. She therefore thought that the symptoms were now prolonged, as she was just a few months shy of 50, the half century marker, and so gave no thought to the virus that was now infecting all age groups with the resultant disease of COVID-19.

COVID-19 does not care who you are. It is no respecter of persons. it loves human beings. It loved Protie too. So in the prime of her useful utility it struck. Just as she was appreciating the realities of her new life, her resilience was threatened. Nonetheless, she gave gratitude and appreciation for her new life. She had achieved fulfillment and balance and her endurance was being

The end of our USEFUL UTILITY

emulated.

For Protie Peckham, cutting ties meant bringing an end to all social and emotional connections to her beloved village of Covidence, but the coronavirus now further dictated cutting ties with her new-found earthly life.

Just like with Protie, there is an end to our own useful utility.

Chapters of Your Life

Shadows and SILHOUETTES ACROSS OUR NEW LIFE

A shadow is a dark area on a bright surface. In life the focus is on the light in our lives. So it was for Protie who, while revelling in her new life, failed to observe that shadows were approaching. The more light, the more shadows, with some overlapping which she even mistook for colours and embraced as "the colours of her dreams".

Like Protie, we are enjoying life's silhouettes instead of fearing them.

"All our days two silhouettes on the shade"...

Our life is the shade. Silhouettes on our life can be compared to youth and maturity, fun and frolic, career and wealth creation, success and failure, health and sickness, death and dying. Occurrences such as the coronavirus, cancer, asthma, diabetes, hypertension, and strokes are examples of shadows that stream across our lives. Silhouettes are created and, like pictures on our walls, we pass them daily – periodically dusting them off without noticing that the colours are fading; that moths are rotting; that decay has set in. So is our life.

In an earlier section of our story, "The Realities of a New Life" (pp. 43-45), we are reminded that: "The realities of a new life force us to look in the rear-view mirror while forging ahead with living our best lives." But the shadows and silhouettes are integral to these realities, and they beg to be recognized. We speak of maladies and leave them hanging – as, for example, "I am diabetic", "I am asthmatic", "I am a cancer survivor", "I have beaten COVID-19", and so on and so forth. All diseases are life threatening; survival brings hope, and planning for an end to our new life is sobering. A single, middle-aged woman such as Protie Peckham ought to have taken heed.

> *Just as in earlier life cycles we reminisced about choices and guidelines for living our new lives, so in our final life cycle of "self-realization" we must also reflect on the shadows and silhouettes as "the sky gets dark, slowly".*

NOTES & COMMENTS

Page

NOTES & COMMENTS

Page

www.ingramcontent.com/pod-product-compliance
Lightning Source LLC
Chambersburg PA
CBHW051709090426
42736CB00013B/2619